# DOLPHIN

BY TYLER GRADY

Dylanna Press

Dolphins are one of the most intelligent and beloved creatures on Earth. They are a species of marine **mammal** that is closely related to whales and porpoises. They belong to the order Cetacea, along with whales, and marine dolphins belong to the family Delphinidae.

There are over 40 different types of dolphins. Some can be found in tropical waters, while others prefer colder climates. Some common species of dolphins include bottlenose, Amazon River, spinner, striped, and hourglass.

---

mammals – warm-blooded animals with hair or fur that give birth to live young

**Dolphins are** graceful, streamlined mammals found in warm waters all around the world. They are one of the most recognizable species of animals.

Dolphins have torpedo-shaped bodies. Their heads are elongated with a beak that is distinct from their snout. They typically weigh between 300 and 600 pounds (135 to 275 kg) and measure 8 to 10 feet (2.4 to 3 meters) in length.

Their bodies are smooth and hairless and they are light to dark gray in color with lighter coloration on their bellies.

They have pectoral fins, or flippers, on either side of their bodies. These flippers help with steering and maneuvering in the water. Their powerful tails are composed of two flukes that help them move fast through the water. A single dorsal fin on their backs provides stability and prevents the dolphin from rolling over.

**Dolphins have** many physical **adaptations** to their environment, which help them to thrive in the ocean. One such adaptation is their body shape, which allows them to move through the water quickly and easily. Another is a thick layer of blubber that helps keep them warm in cold water.

Blubber helps dolphins to **thermoregulate**, which is the ability to maintain a constant body temperature in different environments. Their blubber layer acts like insulation, trapping heat close to their bodies and helping them to stay warm even in cold waters. This blubber also provides **buoyancy**, making it easier for dolphins to rise and sink in the water.

---

**adaptations** – ways in which a species becomes fitted into its natural environment to increase its chance of survival

**thermoregulate** – ability of an organism to maintain its internal body temperature

**buoyancy** – an object's ability to float in water

# Dolphins have an incredible ability to navigate their environment and locate prey with amazing precision—even in the dark! This is through a process known as **echolocation**. Echolocation is a type of biological sonar used by dolphins to produce sound waves that travel through water, bounce off of objects, and echo back to the dolphin's ears.

In addition to being able to detect objects around them, dolphins can also use echolocation for communication with one another. By producing low-frequency clicks, dolphins can transmit information such as location descriptions, predator warnings, and social interactions with other members of their pod.

---

echolocation – use of sound waves for navigation and to locate objects

Dolphins are **carnivores** and their diet consists mainly of fish, squid, octopus, and **crustaceans**. However, they have also been known to feed on other marine creatures like sea turtles, seabirds, and even small sharks depending on the species.

Their diet changes according to the season and availability of food in their **habitat**. An adult dolphin eats 15-30 pounds (6.8 to 13.5 kg) of food per day.

Dolphins find food using their sharp eyesight, acute hearing, and echolocation ability. One sense they don't use is smell—dolphins lack olfactory nerves and cannot smell.

---

carnivore – an animal that only eats meat

crustaceans – animals with hard shells that live in the water such as lobsters and crabs

habitat – surroundings or conditions in which an animal lives

Dolphins are efficient hunters that use a variety of techniques to catch their prey. These include herding, fish whacking, stealth, and ambush tactics.

By working together in pods, dolphins can herd large schools of fish into tight groups. This method allows them to catch more fish—ensuring that there is enough food for everyone!

In fish whacking, dolphins strike their prey with an open flipper or tail, stunning the animal before eating it. These blows are usually delivered from below, taking advantage of the element of surprise as well as momentum from swimming speed.

Stealth hunting involves remaining motionless underwater until an unsuspecting animal swims by—allowing dolphins easy access to their target.

Lastly, ambush tactics involve waiting in hiding until prey come close enough before quickly emerging from cover and attacking.

# Dolphins are **polygamous** and both males and females can have multiple partners in their pod. Breeding takes place year-round. Dolphin pregnancies last between 10 to 18 months depending on the species.

Dolphin babies are called calves. A mother dolphin will give birth to one calf every 2 to 4 years. Baby dolphins are cared for by their mothers, male dolphins do not help raise them. Calves nurse for up to 18 months and stay with their mothers for between 3 to 6 years.

Baby dolphins must quickly learn the skills necessary for surviving in their marine environment including swimming, hunting, and socializing with other members of their pod.

Mothers and calves form strong bonds and may remain in the same pod for life.

---

**polygamous – having more than one mate at a time**

**Like humans,** dolphins need sleep to stay healthy and alert. However, dolphins must always remain at least partially **conscious** so that they stay aware of their surroundings and can surface to breathe. Dolphins have adapted to this need by having only one half of their brains sleep at a time while the other remains partially awake (known as unihemispheric sleep).

Dolphins sleep with one eye open. While one half of the dolphin's brain is asleep, the eye on the opposite side remains open and **vigilant**. They switch between resting sides every couple of hours for a total of about eight hours of sleep per day.

Dolphins are able to swim while sleeping but may rest motionless near the surface.

Dolphin sleeping habits are incredibly complex, yet vital, behaviors that ensure these amazing oxygen-breathing mammals can survive in the ocean!

---

**conscious** – aware, alert, and responsive to environment

**vigilant** – alert and watchful

**Since dolphins** are mammals they need to breathe air into their lungs. Instead of noses, they breathe in air through their blowholes, which are located on the top of their heads. When they come up to the surface, they make a spout of water as they exhale.

Dolphins can't breathe in and out through their mouths—only their blowholes! They close them when they dive underwater so no water gets inside.

Dolphins are able to stay underwater for about 10 minutes (and sometimes as long as 20 minutes) before they need to come up for air.

Dolphins are incredibly social animals, living in tight-knit pods, and forming strong bonds with other members of their group. These bonds are vital for survival as they help dolphins to better locate food sources, alert each other of potential dangers, and even protect one another in times of need!

Dolphins communicate with one another through a wide range of **vocalizations** such as whistles, clicks, and pulsed calls that all carry different meanings. These sounds convey a dolphin's emotions, alert others to the presence of food, and even coordinate cooperative hunting strategies.

Dolphins also rely on body language to communicate. They use tail-slapping, head-butting, breaching (jumping out of the water), and various postures to express themselves without making a sound.

---

**vocalizations – the sounds an animal makes**

The average lifespan of a dolphin in the wild varies by species. The bottlenose dolphin lives for 40-50 years and sometimes longer. River dolphins live around 30 years.

In captivity their lives are much shorter, averaging only 12-15 years. This is due to stress, inferior food, and infections.

There are about 600,000 bottlenose dolphin in the world today. This is the most common species and is not considered threatened. There are currently five species of dolphins that are **endangered**, four of which are river dolphins.

---

**endangered species** – a species that is in danger of becoming extinct

**Dolphins are** near the top of the aquatic **food chain** and it is rare for dolphins to be targeted as prey. However, they are sometimes attacked by large sharks, such as great whites, tiger sharks, and bull sharks.

Other marine animals such as killer whales, seals, and sea lions can also pose a threat to dolphins especially when young or when they are injured.

The biggest danger facing dolphins today is the presence of humans.

---

**food chain – shows how living things get energy from eating other living things**

The most common human-related threats to dolphins come from fishing activities. Getting caught in fishing nets is one of the leading causes of dolphin death worldwide. Being hunted for their meat is another danger. Additionally, noise pollution from boat traffic can disrupt dolphins' ability to communicate with each other and find food sources in their environment. Pollution from industrial runoff may also poison their bodies and affect reproduction rates.

**Climate change** is a major issue affecting all marine life—including dolphins. Increased temperatures reduces food sources and rising sea levels can impact migration and breeding habits.

---

climate change – long-term changes in expected weather patterns

**Dolphins are** incredible animals that captivate us with their intelligence, playful nature, and complex social behaviors. Additionally, dolphins are very curious animals who will often swim up to humans for interaction if given the opportunity. With such an array of wonderful traits it's no wonder that people find dolphins so fascinating.

We hope this book has inspired you to learn more about these incredible animals so that together we can help protect them and ensure their future. Dolphins truly have an extraordinary place in our world!

# Word Search

```
O W C H H B H A B I T A T Y P
T W A V G N I D R E H Y Y I D
H B R R N L B L O W H O L E S
Z U N E D O L P H I N S C L E
S O I L C G S I E E Y L E E S
N Y V S Q H W P C Z K Z T S O
A A O L R Y O B E M A A A L N
E N R E L B I L L C L C C A E
C C E E X I N O O U I S E M L
A Y S P D S F S G C B E A M T
T X U I M Z R E K H A B S A T
S M W N T E R P S H E T E M O
U G X G P O L B K P E W I R B
R N L P M U V X A Y A E K O S
C F I R E H T A E R B N D M N
I L E V A D A P T A T I O N S
F H N O I T A C I N U M M O C
T N I A H C D O O F T K Z R X
```

| | | |
|---|---|---|
| ADAPTATIONS | CETACEA | HABITAT |
| BLOWHOLES | COMMUNICATION | HERDING |
| BLUBBER | CRUSTACEANS | LIFESPAN |
| BOTTLENOSE | DOLPHINS | MAMMALS |
| BREATHE | ECHOLOCATION | SLEEPING |
| BUOYANCY | FLIPPERS | SPECIES |
| CARNIVORES | FOOD CHAIN | THERMOREGULATE |

# INDEX

adaptations, 8
ambush tactics, 15
blowholes, 20
blubber, 8
body language, 23
body shape, 7, 8
bottlenose dolphin, 24
breathing, 19, 20
breeding, 16
buoyancy, 8
calves, 16
captivity, 24
carnivores, 12
Cetacea, 4
climate change, 28
coloration, 7
communication, 11, 23
consciousness, 19
crustaceans, 12
Delphinidae, 4
diet, 12
dorsal fin, 7
echolocation, 11, 12
eyesight, 12
fish herding, 15
fishing activities, 28
fish whacking, 15
flukes, 7
food chain, 27
food sources, 12
habitat, 4, 7, 12
hearing, 12

humans, 27, 28
hunting techniques, 15
intelligence, 4, 31
lifespan, 24
mammals, 4
mating, 16
navigation, 11
noise pollution, 28
parenting, 16
pectoral fins, 7
physical description, 7
pollution, 28
population, 24
porpoises, 4
predators, 27
reproduction, 16
river dolphins, 24
senses, 12
sharks, 27
size, 7
sleep, 19
smell, 12
social interactions, 23
species, 4
stealth hunting, 15
thermoregulation, 8
threats, 27, 28
unihemispheric sleep, 19
vocalizations, 23
weight, 7
whales, 4

Published by Dylanna Press an imprint of Dylanna Publishing, Inc.
Copyright © 2023 by Dylanna Press
Author: Tyler Grady

All rights reserved. No part of this publication may be reproduced, stored in a retrieval system, or transmitted by any means, including electronic, mechanical, photocopying, or otherwise, without prior written permission of the publisher.

Although the publisher has taken all reasonable care in the preparation of this book, we make no warranty about the accuracy or completeness of its content and, to the maximum extent permitted, disclaim all liability arising from its use.

Made in United States
North Haven, CT
17 September 2024